Dear Readers,

Welcome to a culinary journey through the magical season of autumn, where the world is enveloped in a golden haze and the air is filled with the aromas of ripe fruits and fragrant herbs. Autumn, especially the velvet month of September, is a time when nature prepares for winter slumber, offering us its last generous gifts.

For me, autumn has always been a time of year filled with special magic. I fondly remember cozy autumn evenings spent in my grandmother's kitchen. She was a true wizard, capable of turning simple ingredients into culinary masterpieces. As the evenings grew darker and the cold wind pushed fallen leaves around, the house would fill with warmth and the table would be adorned with wonderful dishes infused with the flavors and warmth of autumn.

My grandmother believed that autumn's natural gifts held a special kind of magic. In her hands, pumpkins transformed into soft, fragrant pancakes, and apples baked with cinnamon and honey became soul-soothing desserts. These recipes, passed down through generations, are not just delicious dishes but true spells that bring joy and comfort.

This book is my personal journey back to those days when every autumn meal was filled with special meaning and love. I want to share with you not only the recipes but also the magic contained in each dish. This is an invitation to a world where food becomes a source of health and inspiration, where every meal preparation is a ritual filled with the warmth and gratitude of autumn.

Autumn is a time when the tables are graced with nature's most generous gifts. Each morning at the market, you can find ripe apples, juicy pumpkins, nuts, and fragrant herbs. These products, gathered with care and love, form the foundation for delicious and healthy dishes that my grandmother generously shared with us.

I invite you to join this autumn journey. Here you will find recipes for breakfasts, lunches, and dinners that will warm you and your family on these cool autumn days. Let each recipe be a small spell that can turn an ordinary day into a magical adventure, and each bite remind you of the warmth and care my grandmother put into her dishes.

May these autumn spells bring joy, health, and inspiration into your life. Discover the magic of autumn and let it become part of your culinary creativity as it once became part of mine.

With respect and warmth,
Yurii Sreda

Table of Contents

Introduction: The Magic of Autumn

Foreword

Autumn has always been a time of year when a special kind of magic fills the air. During this period, the world is enveloped in a golden haze, infused with the aromas of ripe fruits and fragrant herbs. Autumn begins with the velvet month of September, when nature prepares for its winter slumber, offering us its final generous gifts.

Since childhood, I have cherished memories of cozy autumn evenings spent in my grandmother's kitchen. She was a true wizard, capable of turning simple ingredients into culinary masterpieces. As darkness fell outside and the cold wind swept fallen leaves, the house would fill with cozy warmth, and the table would be laden with wonderful dishes, filled with the flavors and warmth of autumn.

Grandma used to say that the autumn gifts of nature held a special kind of magic. In her hands, pumpkins would transform into soft, fragrant pancakes, and apples baked with cinnamon and honey became soul-soothing desserts. These recipes, passed down through generations, are not just delicious dishes but true spells capable of bringing joy and comfort.

This book is my personal journey back to those days when every autumn meal was filled with special meaning and love. I want to share with you not only the recipes but also the magic contained in each dish. This is an invitation to a world where food becomes a source of health and inspiration, where every meal preparation becomes a ritual filled with the warmth and gratitude of autumn.

Autumn is a time when the tables are graced with nature's most generous gifts. Every morning at the market, you can find ripe apples, juicy pumpkins, nuts, and fragrant herbs. These products, gathered with care and love, form the foundation for delicious and healthy dishes that my grandmother generously shared with us.

I invite you to join this autumn journey. Here, you will find recipes for breakfasts, lunches, and dinners that will warm you and your family during these cool autumn days. Let each recipe be a small spell capable of turning an ordinary day into a magical adventure, and let each bite remind you of the warmth and care my grandmother put into her dishes.

May these autumn spells bring joy, health, and inspiration into your life. Discover the magic of autumn and let it become a part of your culinary creativity, just as it once became a part of my life.

Autumn Spell

Autumn September is a time when nature reveals its riches in all their glory, bestowing us with generous gifts. It is not just a month of harvest; it is a time when every fruit and vegetable carries the accumulated energy of the summer sun, fresh air, and the life-giving power of the earth. These gifts hold a magic capable of filling life with bright colors and restoring health.

Autumn is a period when our tables are graced with bright, juicy, and healthy products, filled not only with flavor but also with miraculous properties. An autumn spell is the ability to find and use these products so that each meal becomes a true ritual of health and well-being.

When you go to the market in September, it is as if you enter a magical garden where every tree and bush is ready to share its treasures. There are sweet apples, pumpkins of all shapes and sizes, golden pears, bright red tomatoes, and many other gifts that carry the strength and generosity of the autumn earth.

Let's get acquainted with some of these magical ingredients:

- **Pumpkin** — a symbol of autumn, filled not only with flavor but also with nutrients capable of supporting health and giving strength. Pumpkin is rich in vitamins and antioxidants, its bright color absorbing the sun's rays, capable of driving away autumn blues.
- **Apples** — juicy and aromatic, they seem to fill the air with sweetness and warmth. Each bite of an apple is a gulp of health, rich in vitamins and minerals, capable of supporting the immune system and giving vigor.
- **Pears** — sweet and tender, they symbolize abundance and prosperity. Pears, like sunbeams, penetrate our hearts and souls, bringing joy and tranquility.
- **Nuts** — true treasures of autumn, they carry strength and energy, capable of supporting us on cold days. Nuts are rich in healthy fats and proteins, making them an excellent source of energy and health.

- **Honey** — the golden nectar that holds the magic and warmth of summer days. Honey is not only sweet but also beneficial, with antibacterial and anti-inflammatory properties capable of maintaining health and strengthening the immune system.
- **Herbs and spices** — aromatic and spicy, they turn each dish into a true culinary masterpiece. Herbs and spices not only enhance the flavor of food but also bring health benefits, strengthening the body and keeping it in tone.

These ingredients are not just food; they are true magical potions capable of changing our lives for the better. They remind us of the importance of being in harmony with nature, respecting its gifts, and using them wisely and with gratitude.

In this book, I want to share with you the recipes my grandmother taught me to cook. For her, each ingredient was not just a product but a part of a magical ritual capable of filling the home with comfort and joy. She used to say that food prepared with love and care can not only nourish the body but also warm the soul.

I invite you to embark on this autumn journey, where each recipe will become a small spell, and each meal a magical ritual. May the autumn spells fill your life with health and joy, and may the autumn gifts of nature become a source of inspiration and strength.

The Magic of Ingredients

Each ingredient we use in cooking carries not only taste but also magical properties that can affect our health and mood. Autumn September gives us a rich selection of products, each of which holds the power and magic of nature. In this section, I will talk about some of them so you can better understand their unique properties and learn to use them in your culinary spells.

Pumpkin: The Sun of Autumn
Pumpkin is a symbol of autumn that fills our kitchen with bright sunlight. It not only looks beautiful on the table but also has many beneficial properties.

- **Magical properties:** Pumpkin is rich in vitamins A and C, which help strengthen the immune system and improve skin condition. It also contains a lot of fiber, which helps maintain the health of the digestive system.
- **Effect on mood:** Thanks to its bright color and sweet taste, pumpkin can lift your spirits and give a feeling of warmth and coziness.

Apples: The Gift of the Gods
Since ancient times, apples have been considered a symbol of health and longevity. These juicy fruits not only have an excellent taste but also numerous beneficial properties.

- **Magical properties:** Apples are rich in antioxidants and vitamins that help fight inflammation and strengthen the immune system. They also contain pectin, which helps lower cholesterol levels and maintain heart health.
- **Effect on mood:** Fresh and juicy apples give a boost of vigor and energy, improve mood, and help reduce stress.

Pears: The Sweetness of Life

Pears are not only a tasty and healthy fruit but also a symbol of abundance and prosperity. Their delicate sweetness and juiciness make them an indispensable ingredient in autumn dishes.

- **Magical properties:** Pears contain vitamins C and K, as well as many antioxidants that help strengthen the immune system and maintain bone health. The high fiber content helps improve digestion.
- **Effect on mood:** Pears, thanks to their sweet taste, help improve mood and give a feeling of comfort and relaxation.

Nuts: The Power of Nature

Nuts are real natural treasures that contain a huge amount of beneficial substances. They are an excellent source of protein and healthy fats necessary for health and energy.

- **Magical properties:** Nuts are rich in vitamins E and B, as well as magnesium and zinc, which help strengthen the nervous system and improve cognitive functions. Healthy fats help maintain heart and vascular health.
- **Effect on mood:** Nuts help improve concentration and memory, reduce stress levels, and contribute to overall mood improvement.

Honey: The Golden Nectar

Honey is not just a sweet product but also a powerful means of maintaining health. Since ancient times, honey has been used as a natural medicine and source of energy.

- **Magical properties:** Honey has antibacterial and anti-inflammatory properties that help strengthen the immune system and fight infections. It is also rich in antioxidants that slow down the aging process.
- **Effect on mood:** Honey improves mood, helps fight fatigue, and increases vitality. Its sweet taste gives a feeling of joy and comfort.

Herbs and Spices: The Aromas of Magic

Herbs and spices are real natural magicians that can turn the most ordinary dishes into culinary masterpieces. They not only give food a unique taste and aroma but also have numerous beneficial properties.

- **Magical properties:** Spices such as cinnamon, cloves, and ginger have anti-inflammatory and antioxidant properties that help strengthen the immune system and improve overall health. Herbs such as mint, rosemary, and thyme help improve digestion and relieve stress.
- **Effect on mood:** The aromas of herbs and spices can instantly lift your spirits, improve concentration, and create an atmosphere of coziness and tranquility.

These ingredients are true treasures of autumn that can be used in your culinary spells to create delicious and healthy dishes. By using them in your recipes, you will be able not only to enjoy excellent taste but also to improve your health and mood. May the magic of autumn's natural gifts become part of your life and bring you joy and well-being.

Magical Tips for Choosing and Cooking Ingredients

Autumn September is not only a time for harvesting but also an opportunity to enjoy the magic of cooking, where each ingredient, like a magical element, transforms ordinary dishes into true culinary masterpieces. In this section, I will share with you secrets and tips that will help you preserve all the magic and benefits of autumn products, as well as create an atmosphere of coziness and warmth in your kitchen.

Choosing Ingredients: Shopping with Soul
Every dish begins with selecting ingredients. It's important to approach this process with soul, so every culinary creation is filled with energy and joy.

- **Freshness and Seasonality:** Buy only the freshest and seasonal products. The autumn market offers a variety of gifts that fill our diet with vitamins and beneficial substances. Choose fruits and vegetables that have been recently harvested and have retained their freshness.
- **Local Products:** Support local farmers by purchasing products from them. This is not only eco-friendly but also ensures you get the maximum benefit from your food. Locally grown products are filled with the energy and warmth of the native land.
- **Attention to Details:** Pay attention to the appearance of the products. Apples should be smooth and juicy, pumpkins firm and rich in color, and greens fresh and aromatic. It is important to choose products that look healthy and appealing.

2. Preserving Benefits: Respecting Nature's Gifts
Every product carries not only taste qualities but also healing properties. It is important to preserve these benefits during cooking so that dishes are not only tasty but also provide maximum health benefits.

- **Minimal Processing:** Avoid excessive thermal processing of products. Cook vegetables and fruits by steaming or baking them in the oven. This helps preserve the vitamins and beneficial substances that can be destroyed by prolonged heating.
- **Natural Ingredients:** Use only natural seasonings and spices. Herbs and spices not only give dishes a unique flavor but also enrich them with beneficial substances. Use honey instead of sugar, and olive oil instead of refined fats.
- **Slow Cooking:** Slow cooking preserves more beneficial substances and reveals the true taste of products. Use low heat and slow simmering for soups and stews to make them rich and aromatic.

3. The Magic of Flavor: The Art of Combination

Every dish is the result of combining different flavors and aromas. Learn to combine ingredients so that each one reveals its best qualities and adds magic to your culinary creativity.

- **Contrasts and Harmony:** Experiment with contrasting flavors, such as sweetness and acidity, to create a rich and layered taste. For example, add a bit of tart apple to a sweet salad to give it freshness and lightness.
- **Aroma and Texture:** Use spices and herbs to give dishes depth and richness. Combine different textures—crunchy nuts with soft pumpkins or juicy apples with crunchy seeds. This makes dishes interesting and multifaceted.
- **Healthy Alternatives:** Replace harmful ingredients with healthier alternatives. For example, use whole grain flour instead of white, and coconut oil instead of butter. This helps retain flavor while making the dish healthier.

4. Creating Atmosphere: Food as a Ritual

Cooking is not only the process of creating dishes but also a ritual that fills the home with warmth and coziness. Create an atmosphere around you that inspires and brings joy.

- **Cozy and Comfortable:** Cooking should be enjoyable. Create a cozy and comfortable space in the kitchen. Use candles and warm lighting to create an atmosphere of calm and tranquility.
- **Care and Love:** Put your love and care into cooking. Every dish prepared with soul becomes a source of joy and warmth for you and your loved ones.
- **Autumn Details:** Decorate the kitchen with autumn elements—bright leaves, small pumpkins, and nuts. These little details help create an atmosphere of autumn warmth and magic in your kitchen.

Cooking is an art that allows us not only to enjoy the taste but also to take care of our health and well-being. May these tips help you reveal the magic of autumn products and turn each dish into a culinary miracle that brings you joy and satisfaction.

Section I: Autumn Breakfasts

Magical Mornings

Morning is the time when the world is just waking up, when the first rays of the sun penetrate the windows, filling the rooms with soft golden light, and the air is filled with freshness and coolness. It is the morning that sets the tone for the whole day, and how you start it will affect your mood and well-being.

September mornings are a special time when nature paints the sky in warm golden and pink hues, and the earth prepares for the arrival of autumn, filling the air with the aromas of ripe fruits and fragrant herbs. This time of year, the morning seems especially magical, and there is no better way to start the day than with a cozy, nutritious, and healthy breakfast.

Breakfast is a magical spell that starts the day.

As my grandmother used to say, "Breakfast is not just food, it's a magical ritual that awakens strength and charges energy for the whole day." Breakfast not only fills us with energy but also sets a positive mood, helps gather thoughts, and start the new day with a smile.

Why is breakfast so important?

1. **Energy and Vitality**
   After a night's sleep, our body needs to replenish its energy reserves. Breakfast helps restore blood glucose levels, which is necessary for the normal functioning of the brain and muscles. Skipping breakfast can lead to fatigue and reduced performance throughout the day.
2. **Mood Improvement**
   Breakfast promotes the production of happiness hormones such as serotonin, which improves mood

and reduces stress levels. Starting the day with a tasty and healthy breakfast is a surefire way to lift your spirits and set a positive tone.

3. **Metabolism Support**
Regular breakfast helps maintain a high metabolism, which contributes to better nutrient absorption and weight control. Skipping breakfast can slow down metabolism and lead to weight gain.

4. **Concentration and Mental Activity**
Breakfast provides our brain with the necessary nutrients that help improve concentration and cognitive functions. This is especially important for children and adults who have school or work requiring high levels of attention and mental activity.

How to Make Breakfast Magical?

The secret to a magical breakfast lies in the right choice of ingredients and the way they are prepared. It is important to include foods in breakfast that are not only delicious but also beneficial, providing the body with all the necessary nutrients.

1. **Fruits and Berries**
September is the time when apples, pears, and many other fruits are ripe, filling our breakfast with vitamins and antioxidants. Add fresh fruits and berries to your morning diet to get energized and improve your mood.

2. **Whole Grains**
Use whole grain products such as oatmeal, buckwheat, or quinoa. They are rich in fiber and help maintain a feeling of fullness for a long time. Porridge for breakfast is not only delicious but also beneficial for digestion and maintaining healthy blood sugar levels.

3. **Nuts and Seeds**
Add nuts and seeds such as walnuts, almonds, or flaxseeds to your breakfast. They are rich in healthy fats, proteins, and micronutrients that support heart and brain health. Nuts and seeds also give dishes a pleasant texture and rich taste.

4. **Honey and Natural Sweeteners**
Use honey or other natural sweeteners instead of sugar. Honey is not only sweet but also rich in antioxidants and vitamins that support the immune system and improve overall health. Add a little honey to your porridge or toast to add sweetness and benefits to your breakfast.

5. **Herbs and Spices**
Use herbs and spices to enhance the flavor and aroma of dishes. Cinnamon, ginger, mint, and other spices not only give food a unique taste but also have numerous beneficial properties such as improving digestion and boosting immunity.

Examples of Magical Breakfasts

1. **Sunny Pumpkin Pancakes with Cinnamon**
Pumpkin and cinnamon are a magical combination that fills the morning with warmth and coziness. Pumpkin pancakes are not only delicious but also beneficial due to their high content of vitamins and antioxidants.

2. **Honey Apples in Oatmeal**
Sweet and juicy apples combined with oatmeal and honey create a tender and nutritious dish that will energize you for the whole day.

3. **Avocado Toast with Poached Egg and Greens**
Avocado toast with a poached egg and fresh greens is a light and healthy breakfast that provides the body with healthy fats and proteins necessary for a good start to the day.

Let every breakfast become a magical ritual for you, filling the morning with light and joy, and may the autumn spells bring you health and inspiration every day.

Breakfast Recipes

Sunny Pumpkin Pancakes with Cinnamon

Description: Pumpkin and cinnamon pancakes are the perfect autumn dish that fills the morning with warmth and coziness. They turn out airy, soft, and incredibly aromatic. The secret of their magical taste lies in the combination of sweet pumpkin and spicy cinnamon, which create a true autumn symphony of flavors. These pancakes are not only delicious but also healthy, as pumpkin is rich in vitamins and antioxidants.

Ingredients:

- 1 cup pumpkin puree (fresh or canned)
- 1 ½ cups flour
- 1 cup milk (plant-based milk can be used)
- 2 tablespoons sugar
- 1 egg
- 2 tablespoons vegetable oil (e.g., olive or coconut oil)
- 1 teaspoon baking powder
- ½ teaspoon baking soda
- 1 teaspoon cinnamon
- ¼ teaspoon nutmeg (optional)
- A pinch of salt
- Oil for frying

Instructions:

1. **Preparing the Pumpkin Puree:**

o If using fresh pumpkin, it needs to be baked or boiled first. Cut the pumpkin into small pieces, place on a baking sheet, and bake in the oven at 180°C (350°F) for about 20-30 minutes until soft. Then blend or mash with a fork until smooth.

2. **Mixing the Dry Ingredients:**
   o In a large bowl, mix the flour, sugar, baking powder, baking soda, cinnamon, nutmeg, and a pinch of salt. Stir well to evenly distribute all the ingredients.

3. **Preparing the Wet Ingredients:**
   o In another bowl, beat the egg, add milk, vegetable oil, and pumpkin puree. Mix thoroughly until smooth.

4. **Combining the Ingredients:**
   o Gradually add the dry ingredients to the wet ingredients, stirring constantly. Be careful not to overmix—stir until the ingredients are just combined. The batter should be slightly thick but not too dense.

5. **Cooking the Pancakes:**
   o Heat a skillet over medium heat and add a little oil. Spoon the batter onto the skillet, spreading it slightly with a spoon to form round pancakes. Cook the pancakes for 2-3 minutes on each side until golden brown and cooked through.

6. **Serving:**
   o Place the cooked pancakes on a plate lined with paper towels to remove excess oil. Serve them hot, drizzled with honey, maple syrup, or sprinkled with powdered sugar. You can also add some walnuts or fresh berries for garnish and extra flavor.

Cooking Tips:

- You can make the pancakes even more aromatic by adding a bit of vanilla or ginger to the batter.
- For fluffier pancakes, use self-raising flour or add a bit of sparkling water to the batter.

Nutritional Value (per serving):

- Calories: about 150 kcal
- Proteins: 4 g
- Fats: 6 g
- Carbohydrates: 20 g
- Fiber: 2 g

These sunny pumpkin pancakes with cinnamon will give you a true autumn delight and fill your morning with warmth and coziness. Enjoy their flavor with a cup of hot tea or coffee, and let each day begin with the magic of autumn's gifts.

Honey Apples in Oatmeal

Description: Honey apples in oatmeal is the perfect breakfast for an autumn morning. The combination of sweet and juicy apples with honey and the aroma of cinnamon creates an unparalleled taste and fragrance that warms and brings joy. This breakfast is not only delicious but also very healthy: oatmeal provides energy and fiber, while apples and honey boost the immune system and lift the mood.

Ingredients:

- 1 cup rolled oats (not instant)
- 2 cups milk (or plant-based milk)
- 1 large apple
- 2 tablespoons honey
- 1 teaspoon cinnamon
- 1/2 teaspoon vanilla extract (optional)
- A pinch of salt
- Nuts and seeds for garnish (optional)

Instructions:

1. **Cooking the Oatmeal:**
   - In a small saucepan over medium heat, bring the milk to a boil. Add a pinch of salt and the rolled oats. Reduce the heat and simmer, stirring occasionally, for about 5-7 minutes, or until the oats are soft and have absorbed all the liquid.
2. **Preparing the Apples:**
   - While the oatmeal is cooking, peel and core the apple, and cut it into small cubes.
3. **Cooking the Honey Apples:**

- In a small skillet over medium heat, melt one tablespoon of honey. Add the diced apples and sauté for 3-5 minutes, until they are soft and slightly caramelized. Add cinnamon and vanilla extract, stir, and cook for another minute.

4. **Assembling the Dish:**
   - When the oatmeal is ready, remove it from the heat and stir in the remaining tablespoon of honey. Divide the oatmeal into bowls and top with the honey apples.

5. **Garnishing and Serving:**
   - If desired, garnish the oatmeal with nuts and seeds such as walnuts, almonds, or chia seeds. Serve the oatmeal hot with a cup of hot tea or coffee.

Cooking Tips:

- For a richer flavor, you can add a bit of nutmeg or ginger to the oatmeal.
- If you want to make the oatmeal even healthier, add some flaxseeds or chia seeds before serving.

Nutritional Value (per serving):

- Calories: about 250 kcal
- Proteins: 7 g
- Fats: 6 g
- Carbohydrates: 45 g
- Fiber: 5 g

Honey apples in oatmeal are a great way to start the day with warmth and coziness, enjoying the taste of autumn fruits and nutritious oats. Let this breakfast bring you joy and energy for the whole day, filling each morning with the magic of autumn.

Buckwheat Porridge with Nuts and Berries

Description: Buckwheat porridge with nuts and berries is the perfect breakfast for those who value not only taste but also health benefits. Buckwheat is rich in proteins, iron, and B vitamins, making it an excellent source of energy for the whole day. Combined with nuts and fresh berries, it turns into a true culinary wonder, filled with the aroma of autumn and boosting vitality and good mood.

Ingredients:

- 1 cup buckwheat
- 2 cups water
- 1 tablespoon honey
- 1/4 cup chopped nuts (walnuts, almonds, hazelnuts)
- 1/2 cup fresh berries (raspberries, blueberries, strawberries)
- A pinch of salt
- 1 teaspoon cinnamon (optional)
- Milk or yogurt for serving (optional)

Instructions:

1. **Cooking the Buckwheat:**
   - Rinse the buckwheat thoroughly under cold water. In a saucepan, bring the water to a boil, add a pinch of salt, and pour in the buckwheat. Reduce the heat to low, cover, and simmer for 15-20 minutes until all the water is absorbed and the buckwheat is soft.
2. **Preparing the Nuts and Berries:**
   - While the buckwheat is cooking, chop the nuts into small pieces. Rinse and dry the fresh berries.
3. **Mixing the Ingredients:**

- When the buckwheat is ready, add the honey and cinnamon, and mix well. Spoon the buckwheat into a bowl and top with the nuts and berries. You can also drizzle the porridge with milk or add a bit of yogurt for extra creaminess and flavor.

4. **Garnishing and Serving:**
   - Serve the porridge hot, garnished with extra berries and nuts for added beauty and crunch. This dish can be served with a cup of hot tea or coffee.

Cooking Tips:

- For a richer flavor, you can toast the nuts in a dry skillet before adding them to the porridge.
- You can use various berries depending on the season and your taste to add variety and color to your morning dish.

Nutritional Value (per serving):

- Calories: about 300 kcal
- Proteins: 8 g
- Fats: 10 g
- Carbohydrates: 45 g
- Fiber: 7 g

Buckwheat porridge with nuts and berries is not only a delicious and nutritious breakfast but also a true autumn delight. Let this breakfast fill your morning with warmth and energy, giving you a boost of vitality and good mood for the whole day.

Pumpkin Spice Muffins

Description: On a cool autumn morning, when the air is filled with the aroma of spices and fresh baking, there's nothing better than enjoying pumpkin muffins with a cup of hot tea. These muffins seem to have absorbed all the sunny energy of autumn, providing warmth and coziness to everyone who takes a bite. Their tender taste and the aroma of cinnamon, ginger, and nutmeg will fill your home with a sense of magic and comfort.

Ingredients:

- 1 ½ cups flour
- 1 cup pumpkin puree (fresh or canned)
- ½ cup sugar
- 1/3 cup vegetable oil (e.g., olive or coconut oil)
- 2 eggs
- 1 teaspoon baking powder
- ½ teaspoon baking soda
- 1 teaspoon cinnamon
- ½ teaspoon ground ginger
- ¼ teaspoon nutmeg
- A pinch of salt
- ½ cup chopped nuts (optional)
- 1 teaspoon vanilla extract (optional)

Instructions:

1. **Preparing the Oven and Muffin Pan:**
   o Preheat the oven to 180°C (350°F). Grease the muffin pan or line with paper liners.
2. **Mixing the Dry Ingredients:**
   o In a large bowl, mix the flour, sugar, baking powder, baking soda, cinnamon, ginger, nutmeg, and a pinch of salt. Stir well to evenly distribute all the ingredients.
3. **Preparing the Pumpkin Puree:**
   o If using fresh pumpkin, bake or boil it first, then blend or mash with a fork until smooth.
4. **Mixing the Wet Ingredients:**
   o In another bowl, beat the eggs, then add the vegetable oil, pumpkin puree, and vanilla extract. Mix thoroughly until smooth.
5. **Combining the Ingredients:**
   o Gradually add the dry ingredients to the wet ingredients, stirring constantly. If desired, add the chopped nuts to the batter for extra crunch and rich flavor.
6. **Baking the Muffins:**
   o Spoon the batter into the muffin pan, filling each cup about 2/3 full. Place the pan in the preheated oven and bake for 20-25 minutes until the muffins are risen and golden brown. Check for doneness with a wooden stick: if it comes out clean, the muffins are ready.
7. **Cooling and Serving:**
   o Remove the muffins from the oven and let them cool in the pan for a few minutes, then transfer to a wire rack to cool completely. Serve the muffins warm, dusted with powdered sugar or drizzled with honey.

Cooking Tips:

- For a richer flavor, you can add a bit of ground cloves or cardamom to the batter.
- Try adding finely chopped dried fruits such as raisins or apricots to the batter for extra sweetness and texture.

Nutritional Value (per serving):

- Calories: about 180 kcal
- Proteins: 3 g
- Fats: 8 g
- Carbohydrates: 25 g
- Fiber: 2 g

Pumpkin spice muffins are not just a breakfast; they are a little piece of autumn on your table, bringing warmth and the magic of every autumn morning. Let these muffins fill your home with the aroma of spices and the joy of cozy family breakfasts.

Avocado Toast with Poached Egg and Herbs

Description: Avocado toast with poached egg and herbs is the true embodiment of morning magic. It fills the home with the aroma of freshness and greenery, turning an ordinary morning into a small culinary wonder. This breakfast combines health benefits and exquisite taste, reminding us how important it is to start the day with care for ourselves and our loved ones. Soft and creamy avocado, with a tender poached egg, lightly seasoned with herbs and a pinch of love, is the perfect way to start a new day with a feeling of joy and warmth.

Ingredients:

- 1 ripe avocado
- 2 slices whole grain bread
- 2 eggs
- 1 tablespoon white wine vinegar
- 1 tablespoon olive oil
- Salt and pepper to taste
- Fresh herbs (e.g., parsley, dill, or cilantro) for garnish
- A pinch of chili flakes (optional)
- Juice of half a lemon

Instructions:

1. **Preparing the Toast:**
   o Toast the slices of bread in a toaster or on a skillet until golden brown. Drizzle them with olive oil and lightly rub with a garlic clove for aroma (optional).
2. **Preparing the Avocado:**
   o Cut the avocado in half, remove the pit, and scoop out the flesh with a spoon. Mash the avocado with a fork until smooth, add lemon juice, salt, and pepper to taste. Mix thoroughly.

3. **Making Poached Eggs:**
   o In a large saucepan, bring water to a boil. Add a tablespoon of white wine vinegar. Reduce the heat to a gentle simmer. Crack the egg into a small cup. Create a gentle whirlpool in the water with a spoon and carefully pour the egg into the center. Cook the egg for 3-4 minutes until the white is set, but the yolk remains runny. Remove the egg with a slotted spoon and repeat the process with the second egg.
4. **Assembling the Toast:**
   o Spread the mashed avocado on the toasted bread slices. Carefully place the poached egg on top of the avocado. Sprinkle the toast with fresh herbs, chili flakes (optional), and season lightly with salt and pepper.
5. **Serving:**
   o Serve the toasts immediately while they are warm and fresh. They pair perfectly with a cup of hot tea or coffee.

Cooking Tips:

- For extra flavor, you can add a bit of grated garlic or finely chopped onion to the avocado.
- Try adding some fresh tomato or radish to the avocado topping for a variety of flavors and textures.

Nutritional Value (per serving):

- Calories: about 250 kcal
- Proteins: 8 g
- Fats: 18 g
- Carbohydrates: 15 g
- Fiber: 6 g

Avocado toast with poached egg and herbs is not just a breakfast; it's a true work of culinary art that fills the morning with joy and health. Let this breakfast give you strength and inspiration for the whole day, filling every moment with the magic and warmth of an autumn morning.

Berry Smoothie with Nut Milk

Description: An autumn morning, filled with freshness and coolness, holds a special magic. There's nothing better than starting this magical day with a bright and nutritious berry smoothie, which seems to have absorbed all the energy of the autumn garden. The blend of fresh berries and nut milk creates an incredible sense of harmony and warmth, like a morning kiss from the sun breaking through the golden leaves. This smoothie is not only delicious but also rich in vitamins and antioxidants, giving you energy and joy for the entire day.

Ingredients:

- 1 cup fresh or frozen berries (raspberries, blueberries, strawberries, blackberries)
- 1 banana
- 1 cup nut milk (almond, coconut, cashew)
- 1 tablespoon honey or maple syrup (optional)
- 1 tablespoon chia or flax seeds (optional)
- A pinch of vanilla extract (optional)
- A few ice cubes (if using fresh berries)

Instructions:

1. **Preparing the Berries:**
   - If using frozen berries, let them thaw slightly. If using fresh berries, wash and dry them thoroughly. It's important to choose the juiciest and ripest berries to ensure the smoothie is as flavorful and rich as possible.
2. **Preparing the Banana:**
   - Peel the banana and cut it into small pieces. The banana will add natural sweetness and a creamy texture to the smoothie.

3. **Blending the Ingredients:**
   o In a blender, combine the berries, banana, nut milk, honey or maple syrup (if using), chia or flax seeds, and vanilla extract. Blend all the ingredients until smooth. If using fresh berries, add a few ice cubes to make the smoothie cool and refreshing.
4. **Serving:**
   o Pour the smoothie into a tall glass or bowl. Garnish with fresh berries, mint, or chia seeds for added beauty and nutritional benefit.

Cooking Tips:

- For a richer flavor, you can add a bit of fresh ginger or mint to the smoothie.
- Try using different combinations of berries and nut milk to create new flavor variations each time.

Nutritional Value (per serving):

- Calories: about 200 kcal
- Proteins: 4 g
- Fats: 5 g
- Carbohydrates: 35 g
- Fiber: 7 g

A berry smoothie with nut milk is not just a breakfast; it's a true culinary spell that brings joy and freshness to an autumn morning. Let this drink fill your day with energy and health, giving you a sense of warmth and light from the very first sip.

Quinoa with Apples and Cinnamon

Description: On autumn mornings, as the world awakens and the sun begins to light up the earth with its golden rays, it's delightful to enjoy a warm and aromatic breakfast. Quinoa with apples and cinnamon is not just food, but a true journey into a magical autumn garden. The combination of fluffy quinoa, sweet apples, and fragrant cinnamon creates a unique dish that fills the day with energy and joy. This breakfast warms the soul and body, giving the morning ritual a special meaning and warmth.

Ingredients:

- 1 cup quinoa
- 2 cups water or milk (plant-based milk can be used)
- 1 large apple
- 2 tablespoons honey or maple syrup
- 1 teaspoon cinnamon
- 1/4 teaspoon ground ginger (optional)
- A pinch of salt
- 1/4 cup chopped nuts (walnuts, almonds)
- Raisins or dried cranberries (optional) for garnish
- Juice of half a lemon (optional)

Instructions:

1. **Preparing the Quinoa:**
   - Rinse the quinoa under cold water to remove bitterness. In a saucepan, bring the water or milk to a boil, add a pinch of salt, and quinoa. Reduce the heat to low, cover, and simmer for about 15 minutes until all the liquid is absorbed and the quinoa is soft.
2. **Preparing the Apples:**

- Peel and core the apple, then cut it into small cubes. To preserve freshness and flavor, you can drizzle the apple cubes with lemon juice.

3. **Cooking the Quinoa with Apples:**
   - Add the apples, honey or maple syrup, cinnamon, and ginger (if using) to the cooked quinoa. Mix well and let it sit for a few minutes for the flavors to meld together.

4. **Serving:**
   - Divide the quinoa into bowls and garnish with chopped nuts, raisins, or dried cranberries. You can add a bit of honey on top for extra sweetness.

Cooking Tips:

- For a richer flavor and texture, you can add some grated ginger or nutmeg to the quinoa.
- Try using different varieties of apples to get various shades of flavor and aroma.

Nutritional Value (per serving):

- Calories: about 250 kcal
- Proteins: 6 g
- Fats: 8 g
- Carbohydrates: 40 g
- Fiber: 5 g

Quinoa with apples and cinnamon is not just a breakfast; it's a true culinary journey that transports you to an autumn garden filled with aromas and warmth. Let this dish bring you joy and coziness, filling every morning with magic and health.

Section II: Magical Lunches

The Magic of Lunchtime

Lunch is a special moment when we can rest, recharge, and enjoy a delicious meal with family or friends. During the day, as the sun rises higher and illuminates the world with its golden rays, it's time to immerse ourselves in the magic of lunchtime. In autumn, this moment is filled with a unique magic: the aromas of freshly prepared dishes blend with the scents of fallen leaves and warm earth, creating an atmosphere of coziness and tranquility.

Lunchtime is not just a meal; it's a ritual that allows us to pause and savor every moment. It's a time to forget the hustle and bustle and dedicate ourselves to enjoying delicious and healthy food. In autumn, when nature generously offers us its bounty, lunch becomes a true celebration filled with the aromas and flavors of the season.

The Magic of Autumn Lunches: Autumn lunches are more than just food. They are a journey into a world of flavors and aromas that warm the soul and body. Each autumn lunch carries a bit of magic, filling us with energy and joy. During this time of year, when nature provides an abundance of vegetables and fruits, every lunch becomes an opportunity to try something new and wonderful.

Autumn lunches are a time to enjoy the taste of freshly prepared dishes made from the best products that the autumn harvest has to offer. It's an opportunity to try new things, experiment with ingredients and recipes, and enjoy the taste of natural and healthy foods.

Health and Energy: Lunch is not only a tasty meal but also a source of energy and health. It's important to choose dishes that will fill us with strength and support our health. In autumn, when the body needs extra vitamins and minerals, lunchtime dishes should be especially nutritious and beneficial.

- **Vegetables and Greens:** Autumn vegetables are real treasures, filled with vitamins and micronutrients. They help support the immune system and provide the body with essential nutrients. Use pumpkins, zucchini, carrots, cabbage, and other autumn vegetables in your dishes to fill them with freshness and benefits.
- **Proteins and Carbohydrates:** Lunch dishes should contain enough proteins and carbohydrates to provide the body with energy for the entire day. Include legumes, grains, nuts, and seeds in your lunches to maintain high energy levels and satiety.
- **Antioxidants and Vitamins:** Autumn fruits and berries are rich in antioxidants and vitamins that help fight inflammation and support the health of skin and hair. Add apples, pears, cranberries, and other autumn fruits to your dishes to make them even healthier and tastier.

Atmosphere and Coziness: An autumn lunch is not only delicious food but also an atmosphere of coziness and warmth. It's important to create an environment that promotes relaxation and enjoyment of the meal. Decorate your table with autumn decorations like leaves, pumpkins, and candles to create a cozy and magical atmosphere.

- **Cozy Lighting:** Use soft, warm lighting to create a cozy atmosphere at the dining table. Candles or small lamps with warm light will help create a peaceful and comfortable ambiance.
- **Music and Nature Sounds:** Play calming music or nature sounds to create a relaxing atmosphere. This will help you forget about everyday worries and enjoy lunch in a serene and soothing environment.
- **Autumn Scents:** Use aromatic candles or diffusers with scents of cinnamon, apples, and spices to fill the home with cozy and warm autumn aromas. These scents will create a cozy atmosphere and help you relax.

An autumn lunch is not just a meal; it's a true ceremony that allows you to enjoy every moment, feel connected to nature, and fill the day with warmth and joy. Let every autumn lunch be a source of inspiration and happiness, filling life with the magic and wonder of the autumn season.

Magical Lunch Recipes

Pumpkin Soup with Ginger and Coconut Milk

Description: When autumn envelops the earth in golden hues and the cool wind makes us seek warmth and coziness, it's the perfect time to dive into the world of warming and aromatic dishes. Pumpkin soup with ginger and coconut milk is not just a meal; it's a true elixir that will warm you from the inside and fill your day with magic and joy. The sweetness of pumpkin, the spiciness of ginger, and the creaminess of coconut milk create a harmonious combination that reminds of the warmth of home and cozy autumn evenings.

Ingredients:

- 2 pounds pumpkin (peeled and diced) (900 g)
- 1 onion (finely chopped)
- 2 garlic cloves (minced)
- 1 tablespoon fresh ginger (grated)
- 14 oz coconut milk (400 ml)
- 2 cups vegetable or chicken broth (480 ml)
- 2 tablespoons olive oil
- Salt and pepper to taste
- A pinch of ground nutmeg
- Fresh herbs (parsley or cilantro) for garnish
- Pumpkin seeds or nuts for topping (optional)

Instructions:

1. **Preparing the Ingredients:**
   - Peel and dice the pumpkin into small cubes. Finely chop the onion, mince the garlic, and grate the ginger. Prepare all ingredients in advance to make the cooking process quick and easy.
2. **Sautéing the Vegetables:**
   - Heat the olive oil in a large pot over medium heat. Add the onion and garlic, and sauté until soft and golden, about 5 minutes. Then add the ginger and cook for another 1-2 minutes until fragrant.
3. **Cooking the Soup:**
   - Add the pumpkin and broth to the pot. Bring to a boil, then reduce the heat and simmer for 15-20 minutes until the pumpkin is tender. If you prefer a thicker soup, reduce the amount of broth.
4. **Blending and Adding Coconut Milk:**
   - Remove the pot from the heat and let the soup cool slightly. Use a blender to purée the soup until smooth and creamy. Return the pot to low heat, add the coconut milk, and stir well. Season with salt, pepper, and nutmeg to taste.
5. **Serving:**
   - Ladle the soup into bowls. Garnish with fresh herbs and sprinkle with pumpkin seeds or nuts for added flavor and texture. Serve the soup hot with crusty bread or homemade croutons.

Cooking Tips:

- For a richer flavor, you can add a bit of curry powder or cumin for spiciness.
- Try using different types of pumpkin to get various shades of flavor and aroma.

Nutritional Value (per serving):

- Calories: about 250 kcal
- Proteins: 4 g
- Fats: 18 g
- Carbohydrates: 20 g
- Fiber: 4 g

Pumpkin soup with ginger and coconut milk is not just a lunch; it's a true elixir that will warm you and fill your day with warmth and coziness. Let this soup be your faithful companion on cool autumn days, bringing joy and comfort with every sip.

Buckwheat Noodles with Vegetables and Tofu

Description: An autumn day, when the trees are dressed in bright colors and the cool breeze fills the air with freshness, is perfect for a cozy and nutritious lunch. Buckwheat noodles with vegetables and tofu is not just a dish; it's a journey into a magical world of flavors and aromas. This dish combines lightness and richness, filling your day with energy and comfort. The combination of buckwheat noodles, crunchy vegetables, and soft tofu creates a harmony of flavors that remind you of the warmth of home and the coziness of an autumn day.

Ingredients:

- 7 oz buckwheat noodles (soba) (200 g)
- 7 oz tofu (plain or smoked) (200 g)
- 1 red bell pepper
- 1 carrot
- 1 small zucchini
- 1 garlic clove (minced)
- 2 tablespoons soy sauce
- 1 tablespoon sesame oil
- 1 tablespoon vegetable oil (for frying)
- 1 teaspoon fresh ginger (grated)
- Salt and pepper to taste
- Fresh cilantro or parsley for garnish
- Sesame seeds for topping

Instructions:

1. **Cooking the Buckwheat Noodles:**

o   Bring a pot of water to a boil, add a bit of salt, and cook the buckwheat noodles according to the package instructions, usually 5-7 minutes. Once cooked, drain and rinse the noodles with cold water to prevent sticking. Set aside.

2. **Preparing the Vegetables:**
    o   Peel and cut the carrot into thin strips. Slice the red bell pepper into thin strips and cut the zucchini into thin slices. It's important to cut the vegetables into similar sizes for even cooking.

3. **Preparing the Tofu:**
    o   Cut the tofu into 1 cm (1/2 inch) cubes. Heat the vegetable oil in a skillet over medium heat. Fry the tofu until golden on all sides, about 5 minutes. Remove the tofu from the skillet and set aside.

4. **Stir-Frying the Vegetables:**
    o   In the same skillet, heat the sesame oil and add the garlic and ginger. Sauté over medium heat until fragrant, about 1 minute. Add the sliced vegetables and stir-fry for about 5-7 minutes until they are tender but still crisp.

5. **Combining the Ingredients:**
    o   Add the buckwheat noodles and fried tofu to the skillet with the vegetables. Drizzle with soy sauce and mix well to coat all ingredients evenly. Cook for another 2-3 minutes to combine the flavors.

6. **Serving:**
    o   Divide the buckwheat noodles with vegetables and tofu into bowls. Garnish with fresh cilantro or parsley and sprinkle with sesame seeds for added flavor and texture. Serve hot.

Cooking Tips:

*   For a richer flavor, add a bit of chili or garlic sauce to the dish.
*   Try using different vegetables like broccoli or spinach to create your unique flavor combinations.

Nutritional Value (per serving):

*   Calories: about 350 kcal
*   Proteins: 14 g
*   Fats: 12 g
*   Carbohydrates: 45 g
*   Fiber: 6 g

Buckwheat noodles with vegetables and tofu is not just a lunch; it's a true journey into the world of flavors and aromas that will warm you and fill your day with energy and joy. Let this dish be your faithful companion on autumn days, bringing warmth and comfort with every bite.

Autumn Vegetable Stew with Lentils

Description: Autumn brings an abundance of vibrant vegetables and cooler days that make you crave something warm and nourishing. Autumn vegetable stew with lentils is the perfect dish for such an occasion. This aromatic stew fills the home with coziness and warmth, creating an atmosphere that reminds you of the beauty and abundance of the autumn garden. The combination of tender lentils and juicy vegetables creates a harmonious and hearty dish that will delight you with its taste and nutrition.

Ingredients:

- 1 cup red or green lentils (240 ml for UK)
- 1 large carrot
- 1 bell pepper (red or yellow)
- 1 zucchini or squash
- 1 onion
- 2 garlic cloves
- 2 tablespoons tomato paste
- 2 cups vegetable broth (480 ml for UK)
- 1 tablespoon olive oil
- 1 teaspoon dried thyme
- 1 teaspoon dried basil
- 1 teaspoon paprika
- Salt and pepper to taste
- Fresh herbs (parsley or cilantro) for garnish

Instructions:

1. **Preparing the Lentils:**
   o Rinse the lentils under cold water and set aside. It's important to rinse them thoroughly to remove any impurities and give the dish a clean taste.
2. **Preparing the Vegetables:**
   o Peel and dice the carrot. Slice the bell pepper into strips and cut the zucchini into small cubes. Finely chop the onion and mince the garlic. Prepare all the vegetables in advance to make the cooking process quick and easy.
3. **Sautéing the Vegetables:**
   o Heat the olive oil in a large pot over medium heat. Add the onion and garlic, and sauté until soft and golden, about 5 minutes. Then add the carrot and bell pepper, and cook for another 5 minutes until they start to soften.
4. **Adding Zucchini and Lentils:**
   o Add the zucchini and rinsed lentils to the pot. Stir all the ingredients to combine. Add the tomato paste and vegetable broth, and bring to a boil.
5. **Cooking the Stew:**
   o Reduce the heat to low, add the thyme, basil, and paprika. Season with salt and pepper to taste. Cover the pot and simmer the stew on low heat for about 20-25 minutes until the lentils are soft and the vegetables are fully cooked. Stir occasionally to prevent the stew from sticking to the bottom of the pot.
6. **Serving:**
   o Ladle the stew into bowls and garnish with fresh herbs. Serve hot with crusty bread or homemade flatbreads.

Cooking Tips:

- For a richer flavor, add a bit of red wine or balsamic vinegar to the stew.
- Try using different vegetables like eggplant or sweet potatoes to create your unique flavor combinations.

Nutritional Value (per serving):

- Calories: about 280 kcal
- Proteins: 12 g
- Fats: 8 g
- Carbohydrates: 40 g
- Fiber: 10 g

Autumn vegetable stew with lentils is not just a lunch; it's a true culinary journey that will warm you and fill your day with warmth and coziness. Let this dish be your faithful companion on cool autumn days, bringing joy and comfort with every bite.

Baked Apples with Honey and Nuts

Description: As autumn days give way to cool evenings and the first lights begin to twinkle, it's the perfect time to enjoy something warm and cozy. Baked apples with honey and nuts are not just a dessert; they are a culinary spell that transports you to a world of sweet aromas and magical flavors. The combination of soft, baked apples, sweet honey, and crunchy nuts creates a harmony that warms the soul and brings a sense of peace and joy.

Ingredients:

- 4 large apples
- 4 tablespoons honey
- 1/2 cup chopped nuts (walnuts, almonds, hazelnuts) (120 ml for UK)
- 2 tablespoons raisins or dried cranberries (optional)
- 1 teaspoon cinnamon
- 1/2 teaspoon ground nutmeg (optional)
- 1 tablespoon butter
- Juice of half a lemon

Instructions:

1. **Preparing the Apples:**
   - Preheat the oven to 350°F (180°C). Wash the apples and carefully core them, leaving the bottom intact to create a small well for the filling. Drizzle the apples with lemon juice to prevent browning.
2. **Preparing the Filling:**

- In a small bowl, mix the chopped nuts, raisins or dried cranberries (if using), cinnamon, and nutmeg. Add the honey and mix thoroughly to coat all the ingredients evenly with honey.

3. **Filling the Apples:**
   - Stuff each apple with the prepared mixture, pressing down slightly to pack the filling. Place the apples in a baking dish.

4. **Baking the Apples:**
   - Top each apple with a small piece of butter. Cover the baking dish with foil and bake in the preheated oven for about 25-30 minutes until the apples are soft. Remove the foil and bake for an additional 5-10 minutes until the tops are slightly caramelized.

5. **Serving:**
   - Remove the apples from the oven and let them cool slightly. Serve warm, drizzled with additional honey and garnished with fresh herbs or extra nuts for added flavor and presentation.

Cooking Tips:

- For a richer flavor, add a bit of grated ginger or vanilla to the filling.
- Try using different apple varieties to create unique flavor and texture combinations.

Nutritional Value (per serving):

- Calories: about 200 kcal
- Proteins: 2 g
- Fats: 10 g
- Carbohydrates: 30 g
- Fiber: 4 g

Baked apples with honey and nuts are not just a dessert; they are a true culinary spell that will warm you and fill your day with warmth and coziness. Let this dish be your faithful companion on cool autumn days, bringing joy and comfort with every bite.

Quinoa Salad with Nuts and Pomegranate

Description: When autumn leaves swirl in the air and the sun gently warms the earth, it's the perfect time to enjoy a fresh and nutritious lunch. Quinoa salad with nuts and pomegranate is not just a dish; it's a true celebration of flavors and textures that fills the day with joy and energy. The lightness and healthiness of quinoa combine with crunchy nuts and juicy pomegranate seeds, creating a harmony that reminds us of the beauty and abundance of autumn.

Ingredients:

- 1 cup quinoa (240 ml for UK)
- 2 cups water or vegetable broth (480 ml for UK)
- 1 pomegranate (seeds)
- 1/2 cup toasted and chopped walnuts (120 ml for UK)
- 1/4 cup pumpkin seeds (optional) (60 ml for UK)
- 1 small red onion (finely chopped)
- 1/4 cup fresh parsley (chopped) (60 ml for UK)
- 1/4 cup fresh mint (chopped) (60 ml for UK)
- 1/4 cup olive oil (60 ml for UK)
- Juice of 1 lemon
- Salt and pepper to taste

Instructions:

1. **Cooking the Quinoa:**
   - Rinse the quinoa under cold water. In a saucepan, bring the water or vegetable broth to a boil, add a pinch of salt, and quinoa. Reduce the heat to low, cover, and simmer for about 15 minutes until all the liquid is absorbed and the quinoa is tender. Remove from heat and let cool.

2. **Preparing the Ingredients:**
   o While the quinoa cools, deseed the pomegranate. Toast the walnuts in a dry skillet until golden, then cool and chop them. Finely chop the red onion, parsley, and mint.
3. **Mixing the Ingredients:**
   o In a large bowl, combine the cooled quinoa, pomegranate seeds, chopped walnuts, pumpkin seeds (if using), red onion, parsley, and mint. Mix well to distribute all the ingredients evenly.
4. **Making the Dressing:**
   o In a small bowl, mix the olive oil, lemon juice, salt, and pepper. Whisk until well combined.
5. **Tossing the Salad:**
   o Drizzle the dressing over the salad and gently toss to combine. Let the salad sit for 10-15 minutes to allow the flavors to meld.
6. **Serving:**
   o Serve the salad on plates, either chilled or at room temperature. This salad is perfect as a standalone dish or as a side to main courses.

Cooking Tips:

- For a more intense flavor, add some grated ginger or orange zest to the salad.
- Experiment with different types of nuts and seeds to create your unique flavor and texture combinations.

Nutritional Value (per serving):

- Calories: about 300 kcal
- Proteins: 8 g
- Fats: 16 g
- Carbohydrates: 35 g
- Fiber: 6 g

Quinoa salad with nuts and pomegranate is not just a lunch; it's a true culinary adventure that will warm you and fill your day with joy and energy. Let this dish be your faithful companion on cool autumn days, bringing happiness and comfort with every bite.

Stuffed Peppers with Quinoa and Vegetables

Description: An autumn day, when leaves fall in golden waves and the air is filled with freshness, is perfect for creating a cozy and nutritious lunch. Stuffed peppers with quinoa and vegetables are a true culinary masterpiece that combines vibrant colors, rich aromas, and healthy ingredients. This dish is not only delicious but also beautiful, filling your home with warmth and joy.

Ingredients:

- 4 large sweet peppers (red, yellow, or orange)
- 1 cup quinoa (240 ml for UK)
- 2 cups water or vegetable broth (480 ml for UK)
- 1 medium onion (finely chopped)
- 2 garlic cloves (minced)
- 1 carrot (grated)
- 1 zucchini (diced)
- 1 can (14 oz/400 g) diced tomatoes
- 1 teaspoon dried oregano
- 1 teaspoon dried basil
- 1/2 cup grated cheese (mozzarella or Parmesan) (120 ml for UK)
- 2 tablespoons olive oil
- Salt and pepper to taste
- Fresh parsley for garnish

Instructions:

1. **Cooking the Quinoa:**

- Rinse the quinoa under cold water. In a saucepan, bring the water or vegetable broth to a boil, add a pinch of salt, and quinoa. Reduce the heat to low, cover, and simmer for about 15 minutes until all the liquid is absorbed and the quinoa is tender. Remove from heat and let cool.

2. **Preparing the Peppers:**
   - Preheat the oven to 350°F (180°C). Wash the peppers, cut them in half, and remove the seeds and membranes. Place the peppers on a baking sheet greased with olive oil.

3. **Making the Filling:**
   - In a large skillet, heat the remaining olive oil over medium heat. Add the onion and garlic, and sauté until soft and golden, about 5 minutes. Add the grated carrot and diced zucchini, and cook for another 5-7 minutes until the vegetables are tender.
   - Add the diced tomatoes, dried oregano, basil, salt, and pepper. Stir and cook over medium heat for another 10 minutes until all the ingredients are well combined. Add the cooked quinoa and mix thoroughly.

4. **Stuffing the Peppers:**
   - Fill each pepper half with the prepared filling. Sprinkle grated cheese on top and place the peppers back on the baking sheet.

5. **Baking the Peppers:**
   - Bake the peppers in the preheated oven for about 25-30 minutes until the peppers are soft and the cheese is melted and golden.

6. **Serving:**
   - Remove the peppers from the oven and let them cool slightly. Serve hot, garnished with fresh parsley. These peppers pair perfectly with green salads or crusty bread.

Cooking Tips:

- For a richer flavor, add some fresh herbs like thyme or rosemary to the filling.
- Try using different types of cheese to create your unique flavor combinations.

Nutritional Value (per serving):

- Calories: about 320 kcal
- Proteins: 10 g
- Fats: 12 g
- Carbohydrates: 40 g
- Fiber: 8 g

Stuffed peppers with quinoa and vegetables are not just a lunch; they are a true culinary adventure that will warm you and fill your day with joy and energy. Let this dish be your faithful companion on cool autumn days, bringing warmth and comfort with every bite.

Description: As leaves slowly fall from the trees, painting the ground in golden and red hues, it's the perfect time to create something special that warms and reminds you of the beauty of autumn. An autumn vegetable tart with goat cheese and rosemary is not just a dish; it's a true celebration of flavors and aromas. The crispy crust, tender autumn vegetables, aromatic goat cheese, and fresh rosemary create a harmony that brings joy and coziness to every autumn day.

Ingredients:

- **For the crust:**
    - 1 1/2 cups whole wheat flour (360 ml for UK)
    - 1/2 cup cold butter (cut into cubes) (120 ml for UK)
    - 1/4 cup ice water (60 ml for UK)
    - A pinch of salt
- **For the filling:**
    - 1 large sweet potato (peeled and thinly sliced)
    - 1 small zucchini (thinly sliced)
    - 1 red onion (sliced into rings)
    - 7 oz goat cheese (crumbled) (200 g)
    - 2 tablespoons olive oil
    - 1 teaspoon fresh rosemary (chopped)
    - Salt and pepper to taste

Instructions:

1. **Preparing the Crust:**

- In a large bowl, combine the whole wheat flour and a pinch of salt. Add the cold butter cubes and mix with your hands or a mixer until the mixture resembles coarse crumbs.
- Gradually add the ice water, mixing continuously until the dough begins to come together. Form the dough into a ball, wrap it in plastic wrap, and refrigerate for at least 30 minutes.

2. **Preparing the Vegetables:**
   - While the dough is chilling, preheat the oven to 350°F (180°C). Peel and thinly slice the sweet potato, zucchini, and red onion. Spread the vegetables on a baking sheet, drizzle with olive oil, and season with salt and pepper. Roast in the oven for about 20 minutes until the vegetables are soft.

3. **Assembling the Tart:**
   - Remove the dough from the refrigerator and roll it out on a lightly floured surface to about 1/4 inch (5 mm) thick. Transfer the dough to a tart pan, gently pressing it into the bottom and up the sides. Trim any excess dough from the edges.
   - Evenly distribute the roasted vegetables over the tart crust. Sprinkle the crumbled goat cheese and chopped rosemary on top.

4. **Baking the Tart:**
   - Bake the tart in the preheated oven for about 25-30 minutes until the crust is golden and the cheese is melted and slightly browned.

5. **Serving:**
   - Remove the tart from the oven and let it cool slightly before slicing. Serve warm, garnished with fresh rosemary sprigs and a light drizzle of olive oil.

Cooking Tips:

- For a richer flavor, add some minced garlic or grated ginger to the filling.
- Try using different types of cheese, such as feta or Parmesan, to create your unique flavor combinations.

Nutritional Value (per serving):

- Calories: about 350 kcal
- Proteins: 10 g
- Fats: 20 g
- Carbohydrates: 30 g
- Fiber: 5 g

Autumn vegetable tart with goat cheese and rosemary is not just a lunch; it's a true culinary journey that will warm you and fill your day with joy and coziness. Let this dish be your faithful companion on cool autumn days, bringing warmth and comfort with every bite.

Section III: Magical Dinners

Evening Spells

An autumn evening is a time when the world is bathed in quiet and calm twilight glow, and the air is filled with the coolness and aromas of fallen leaves. It is the time of day when you want to warm up by the hearth, surrounded by coziness and warmth, and enjoy a delicious dinner with family or friends. Evening spells are more than just a meal; they are a ritual that helps end the day on a high note, filling it with harmony and tranquility.

The Magic of Autumn Dinners: In the evening, as the sun slowly sets beyond the horizon and the first stars light up the sky, it's a time for magic and enchantment. Autumn dinners are more than just food. They are moments when you can let go of the day's worries and troubles, immerse yourself in a cozy atmosphere, and savor the aromas and flavors that nature offers us in this beautiful season.

An autumn dinner is an opportunity to create something special that fills the home with warmth and joy. It's a chance to share these moments with loved ones, to feel unity and harmony. In this season, when the harvest brings us an abundance of vegetables, fruits, and aromatic herbs, every dinner becomes a true celebration, full of variety and richness.

Health and Harmony: Autumn dinners are not only delicious but also healthy. It's important to choose dishes that are not only enjoyable to eat but also support health, filling the body with essential vitamins and minerals.

- **Healthy Ingredients:** Include seasonal vegetables and fruits in your dinners, such as pumpkin, zucchini, beets, and apples. They are rich in vitamins, antioxidants, and fiber, which are essential for maintaining health in the autumn season.

- **Balance and Variety:** Aim for balance in your dishes. Combine proteins, fats, and carbohydrates to provide the body with all the necessary nutrients. Use a variety of protein sources, such as fish, poultry, legumes, and nuts.
- **Spices and Herbs:** Autumn is a time for spices. Add cinnamon, ginger, nutmeg, rosemary, and thyme to your dishes to give them a deep and rich flavor. Spices not only enhance the taste but also have numerous health benefits, such as improving digestion and boosting the immune system.

Cozy Atmosphere: An autumn dinner is not just about food; it's also about the atmosphere. It's important to create an environment that promotes relaxation and enjoyment of every moment.

- **Cozy Lighting:** Use candles, warm light lamps, or string lights to create a soft and cozy lighting at the dinner table. This will help you relax and create an atmosphere of peace and comfort.
- **Music and Nature Sounds:** Play calm music or nature sounds to create a relaxing atmosphere. This will help you forget about the hustle and bustle and enjoy dinner in a serene setting.
- **Autumn Scents:** Use scented candles or diffusers with aromas of cinnamon, apples, and spices to fill the home with cozy and warm autumn scents. These aromas will create a cozy atmosphere and help you relax.

An autumn dinner is more than just a meal; it's a true ceremony that allows you to savor every moment, feel connected to nature, and fill the evening with warmth and joy. Let each autumn dinner be a source of inspiration and happiness, filling your life with the magic and enchantment of the autumn season.

Recipes for Dinners

Baked Fish with Lemon and Herbs

Description: On a cool autumn evening, when the wind whispers tales among the golden and scarlet leaves, you crave something that warms and fills the soul with peace. Baked fish with lemon and herbs is not just a dinner; it's a true spell that fills the home with the aromas of the sea and forest. The tender fish fillet, infused with the freshness of lemon and the aroma of fragrant herbs, creates a harmony that turns an ordinary evening into a magical ritual.

Ingredients:

- 4 fillets of white fish (such as cod, pike-perch, or hake)
- 2 lemons (1 sliced thinly, 1 for juice)
- 3 tablespoons olive oil
- 2 tablespoons fresh parsley (chopped)
- 2 tablespoons fresh dill (chopped)
- 2 garlic cloves (minced)
- Salt and pepper to taste
- A pinch of dried thyme (optional)
- Fresh herbs for garnish

Instructions:

1. **Preparing the Fish:**

o Preheat the oven to 400°F (200°C). Rinse the fish fillets and pat them dry with paper towels. Season the fish with salt and pepper on both sides.

2. **Making the Marinade:**
   o In a small bowl, mix the olive oil, juice of one lemon, minced garlic, chopped parsley, and dill. Add a pinch of dried thyme if using. Mix thoroughly.

3. **Marinating the Fish:**
   o Place the fish fillets in a baking dish and pour the prepared marinade over them. Arrange the thin lemon slices on top of the fillets. Let the fish sit in the marinade for about 15-20 minutes to absorb the flavors.

4. **Baking the Fish:**
   o Bake the fish in the preheated oven for about 20-25 minutes until it is tender and flakes easily with a fork. Be careful not to overcook the fish to keep it juicy.

5. **Serving:**
   o Remove the fish from the oven and let it cool slightly. Serve hot, garnished with fresh herbs and the remaining lemon slices. This dish pairs beautifully with a light salad of fresh vegetables or roasted vegetables.

Cooking Tips:

- For a richer flavor, add some grated ginger or a pinch of red pepper to the marinade for a bit of heat.
- Try using different fresh herbs like basil or cilantro to create your unique flavor combinations.

Nutritional Value (per serving):

- Calories: about 220 kcal
- Proteins: 25 g
- Fats: 12 g
- Carbohydrates: 3 g
- Fiber: 1 g

Baked fish with lemon and herbs is not just a dinner; it's a culinary spell that brings lightness and freshness to the evening meal. Let this dish be your faithful companion on cool autumn evenings, filling your home with aromas and warmth.

Chicken with Nut Crust and Vegetables

Description: When the autumn wind rustles the golden leaves and the evening sky is painted in warm hues, you crave something that will warm and nourish, providing a sense of coziness and peace. Chicken with nut crust and vegetables is not just a dinner; it's a magical spell that fills the home with the aromas of spices and fresh herbs. Tender chicken meat in a crispy nut crust, surrounded by juicy autumn vegetables, creates a harmony of flavors and textures that turn an ordinary evening into an unforgettable culinary adventure.

Ingredients:

- 4 chicken breasts
- 1/2 cup chopped nuts (walnuts, almonds, or cashews) (120 ml for UK)
- 1/4 cup breadcrumbs (60 ml for UK)
- 1/4 cup grated Parmesan (60 ml for UK)
- 2 tablespoons olive oil
- 2 garlic cloves (minced)
- 1 tablespoon fresh rosemary (chopped)
- Salt and pepper to taste
- 2 carrots (sliced)
- 1 sweet potato (diced)
- 1 red bell pepper (sliced)
- 1 zucchini (sliced)

Instructions:

1. **Preparing the Chicken:**

o Preheat the oven to 400°F (200°C). Rinse the chicken breasts and pat them dry with paper towels. Season the chicken with salt and pepper on both sides.

2. **Making the Nut Crust:**
   o In a small bowl, mix the chopped nuts, breadcrumbs, grated Parmesan, minced garlic, and fresh rosemary. Add the olive oil and mix well to combine all the ingredients evenly.

3. **Coating the Chicken:**
   o Place the chicken breasts on a baking sheet lined with parchment paper. Generously coat each breast with the nut and breadcrumb mixture, pressing gently to ensure the crust adheres well.

4. **Preparing the Vegetables:**
   o In a large bowl, toss the sliced vegetables with a little olive oil, salt, and pepper. Arrange the vegetables around the chicken breasts on the baking sheet.

5. **Baking the Chicken and Vegetables:**
   o Bake the chicken and vegetables in the preheated oven for about 25-30 minutes until the chicken is golden and juicy and the vegetables are tender and fragrant. Check the doneness of the chicken by cutting into one breast; the juices should run clear.

6. **Serving:**
   o Remove the chicken and vegetables from the oven and let them cool slightly. Serve hot, garnished with fresh herbs such as parsley or basil. This dish pairs beautifully with rice or mashed potatoes.

Cooking Tips:

- For a richer flavor, add some grated lemon zest to the nut mixture.
- Try using different types of nuts to create your unique flavor and texture combinations.

Nutritional Value (per serving):

- Calories: about 450 kcal
- Proteins: 35 g
- Fats: 20 g
- Carbohydrates: 30 g
- Fiber: 5 g

Chicken with nut crust and vegetables is not just a dinner; it's a culinary adventure that will warm you and fill the evening with the aromas and flavors of the autumn forest. Let this dish be your faithful companion on cool autumn evenings, bringing joy and coziness with every bite.

Autumn Pilaf with Pumpkin and Pine Nuts

Description: An autumn evening, when darkness falls earlier and the air is filled with the cool scent of fallen leaves, is the perfect time for cozy and warming dishes. Autumn pilaf with pumpkin and pine nuts is not just a dinner; it's a journey into a fairy tale where every bite is filled with magic. Bright pumpkin, tender pine nuts, and aromatic spices create a harmony that will transport you to Eastern tales and fill your home with warmth and comfort.

Ingredients:

- 1 cup long-grain rice (e.g., basmati or jasmine) (240 ml for UK)
- 300 g pumpkin (peeled and diced)
- 1 onion (finely chopped)
- 2 garlic cloves (minced)
- 1 carrot (grated)
- 1/4 cup pine nuts (60 ml for UK)
- 2 tablespoons olive oil
- 1 teaspoon turmeric
- 1 teaspoon ground coriander
- 1/2 teaspoon cinnamon
- 2 cups vegetable broth (480 ml for UK)
- Salt and pepper to taste
- Fresh parsley for garnish

Instructions:

1. **Preparing Ingredients:**

- Rinse the rice under cold water until the water runs clear. Set aside. Peel and dice the pumpkin, finely chop the onion, mince the garlic, and grate the carrot.

2. **Sautéing Vegetables:**
   - In a large skillet or pot, heat the olive oil over medium heat. Add the onion and sauté until soft and golden, about 5 minutes. Add the garlic and cook for another minute until fragrant.

3. **Adding Rice and Spices:**
   - Add the rice to the skillet and stir for about 2 minutes to coat the grains in the oil and spices. Add the turmeric, ground coriander, and cinnamon, and mix well.

4. **Cooking the Pilaf:**
   - Add the grated carrot and diced pumpkin to the skillet. Stir to distribute the vegetables evenly. Pour in the vegetable broth, bring to a boil, then reduce the heat and cover. Simmer for about 18-20 minutes until the rice is tender and has absorbed all the liquid.

5. **Adding Pine Nuts:**
   - In a small dry skillet, toast the pine nuts over medium heat until golden, about 3-4 minutes. Be careful not to over-toast the nuts.

6. **Finishing the Dish:**
   - When the pilaf is ready, remove it from the heat and let it sit, covered, for another 5 minutes. Spoon the pilaf onto plates, sprinkle with toasted pine nuts, and garnish with fresh parsley.

Cooking Tips:

- For a richer flavor, add some raisins or dried apricots to the pilaf.
- Try using different types of nuts, such as almonds or hazelnuts, to create your unique flavor and texture combinations.

Nutritional Value (per serving):

- Calories: about 320 kcal
- Proteins: 6 g
- Fats: 12 g
- Carbohydrates: 45 g
- Fiber: 4 g

Autumn pilaf with pumpkin and pine nuts is not just a dinner; it's a culinary journey that will warm you and fill the evening with the aromas of Eastern spices and autumn harvests. Let this dish be your faithful companion on cool autumn evenings, bringing joy and comfort with every bite.

Warm Spinach Salad with Pine Nuts

Description: When the autumn evening fills the air with coolness and the aroma of fallen leaves, it's the perfect time for a warm, comforting salad that not only satisfies but also provides a sense of coziness and peace. Warm spinach salad with pine nuts is not just a dish; it's a symphony of flavors and textures. Tender spinach leaves, crunchy pine nuts, and sweet notes of caramelized onion create a harmony that will transport you to a world of magical autumn evenings.

Ingredients:

- 200 g fresh spinach
- 1 red onion (thinly sliced)
- 2 tablespoons pine nuts
- 1 tablespoon olive oil
- 1 tablespoon balsamic vinegar
- 1 teaspoon honey
- Salt and pepper to taste
- A pinch of ground cinnamon (optional)
- 50 g goat cheese (crumbled)
- 1 garlic clove (minced)

Instructions:

1. **Preparing the Ingredients:**
   - Wash and dry the spinach leaves. Thinly slice the red onion. Prepare the remaining ingredients to have everything ready at hand.
2. **Caramelizing the Onion:**

o In a large skillet, heat the olive oil over medium heat. Add the sliced onion and cook, stirring occasionally, for about 10 minutes until the onion is soft and caramelized. Add the honey and balsamic vinegar, and cook for another 2-3 minutes until the onion absorbs all the flavors. Remove from heat and set aside.

3. **Toasting the Pine Nuts:**
   o In a small dry skillet, toast the pine nuts over medium heat until golden, about 3-4 minutes. Be careful not to over-toast the nuts. Remove from heat and set aside.

4. **Cooking the Spinach:**
   o In the same large skillet where the onion was cooked, add the minced garlic and cook over medium heat for about 1 minute until fragrant. Add the spinach and cook, stirring, for about 2-3 minutes until the spinach is wilted and slightly softened. Season with salt, pepper, and a pinch of cinnamon (if using).

5. **Assembling the Salad:**
   o In a large bowl, combine the cooked spinach, caramelized onion, and toasted pine nuts. Sprinkle with crumbled goat cheese. Toss gently to ensure all ingredients are evenly distributed.

6. **Serving:**
   o Divide the salad among plates and serve warm. This salad pairs beautifully with slices of whole grain bread or crunchy crackers.

Cooking Tips:

- For a richer flavor, add some dried cranberries or raisins to the salad.
- Try using different types of nuts, such as walnuts or almonds, to create your unique flavor and texture combinations.

Nutritional Value (per serving):

- Calories: about 250 kcal
- Proteins: 8 g
- Fats: 18 g
- Carbohydrates: 15 g
- Fiber: 4 g

Warm spinach salad with pine nuts is not just a dinner; it's a culinary spell that will warm you and fill the evening with the aromas and flavors of autumn. Let this dish be your faithful companion on cool autumn evenings, bringing joy and comfort with every bite.

Buckwheat with Mushrooms and Nuts

Description: An autumn evening, with the air filled with freshness and leaves rustling underfoot, calls for a warm and cozy dinner. Buckwheat with mushrooms and nuts is not just a dish; it's an immersion into a woodland fairy tale. The rich aroma of mushrooms, the crunch of nuts, and the tender texture of buckwheat create a harmony that transports you to an autumn forest, where every bite fills you with warmth and comfort.

Ingredients:

- 1 cup buckwheat
- 200 g fresh mushrooms (champignons, porcini, or a mix)
- 1 onion (finely chopped)
- 2 garlic cloves (minced)
- 1 carrot (grated)
- 1/2 cup walnuts (toasted and chopped)
- 2 tablespoons olive oil
- 2 cups vegetable broth or water
- Salt and pepper to taste
- Fresh parsley for garnish

Instructions:

1. **Preparing the Buckwheat:**
   o Rinse the buckwheat under cold water. In a saucepan, bring the vegetable broth or water to a boil, add a pinch of salt and the buckwheat. Reduce the heat to low, cover, and cook for about 15 minutes, until the buckwheat is soft and has absorbed all the liquid. Remove from heat and let it sit, covered, for another 5 minutes.
2. **Cooking the Mushrooms and Vegetables:**

- While the buckwheat is cooking, heat the olive oil in a large skillet over medium heat. Add the chopped onion and garlic, and sauté until soft and golden, about 5 minutes. Add the grated carrot and cook for another 2-3 minutes.
3. **Sautéing the Mushrooms:**
   - Slice the mushrooms thinly and add them to the skillet with the vegetables. Cook, stirring, for about 5-7 minutes, until the mushrooms are soft and golden. Season with salt and pepper to taste.
4. **Combining the Ingredients:**
   - Add the cooked buckwheat to the skillet with the mushrooms and vegetables. Stir to combine all ingredients evenly. Add the toasted and chopped walnuts, and mix thoroughly.
5. **Serving:**
   - Divide the buckwheat with mushrooms and nuts among plates. Garnish with fresh parsley and serve hot. This dish pairs beautifully with a green salad or grilled vegetables.

Cooking Tips:

- For a richer flavor, add some fresh thyme or rosemary to the dish.
- Try using different types of nuts, such as almonds or hazelnuts, to create your unique flavor and texture combinations.

Nutritional Value (per serving):

- Calories: about 350 kcal
- Proteins: 10 g
- Fats: 15 g
- Carbohydrates: 40 g
- Fiber: 7 g

Buckwheat with mushrooms and nuts is not just a dinner; it's a culinary adventure that will warm you up and fill the evening with the aromas of an autumn forest. Let this dish be your faithful companion on cool autumn evenings, bringing joy and coziness with every bite.

Pumpkin Pasta with Nut Sauce

Description: An autumn evening, when leaves fall in golden swirls and the air is filled with the scent of spices, is the perfect time for a warm and cozy dinner. Pumpkin pasta with nut sauce is not just a dish; it's true culinary magic. Tender pumpkin, creamy nut sauce, and the aroma of fresh herbs create a harmony that will transport you to an enchanting Italian autumn garden, where each bite fills your heart with warmth and joy.

Ingredients:

- 400 g (14 oz) pasta (such as fettuccine or linguine)
- 300 g (10.5 oz) pumpkin (peeled and cubed)
- 1 onion (finely chopped)
- 2 garlic cloves (minced)
- 1/2 cup toasted walnuts (chopped)
- 1 cup cream (or coconut milk for a vegan option)
- 2 tablespoons olive oil
- 1/4 cup grated Parmesan (optional)
- Salt and pepper to taste
- A pinch of nutmeg
- Fresh herbs (parsley or basil) for garnish

Instructions:

1. **Roasting the Pumpkin:**
   - Preheat the oven to 200°C (400°F). Spread the cubed pumpkin on a baking sheet, drizzle with olive oil, and season with salt and pepper. Roast in the preheated oven for about 20-25 minutes, until the pumpkin is soft and golden.
2. **Cooking the Pasta:**

- In a large pot, bring salted water to a boil and cook the pasta according to package instructions until al dente. Drain the pasta, reserving some cooking water for the sauce.

3. **Making the Nut Sauce:**
   - In a skillet, heat the olive oil over medium heat. Add the finely chopped onion and garlic, and sauté until soft and golden, about 5 minutes. Add the chopped walnuts and cook for another 2-3 minutes until the nuts are fragrant.

4. **Combining the Ingredients:**
   - Add the roasted pumpkin to the skillet with the onion, garlic, and nuts. Stir in the cream (or coconut milk) and bring to a gentle boil. Reduce the heat and simmer for another 5-7 minutes until the sauce is thick and creamy. Season with salt, pepper, and a pinch of nutmeg.

5. **Mixing with the Pasta:**
   - Add the cooked pasta to the skillet with the pumpkin sauce. Toss to coat the pasta evenly with the sauce. If the sauce is too thick, add a little of the reserved pasta cooking water.

6. **Serving:**
   - Divide the pumpkin pasta among plates. Sprinkle with grated Parmesan (if using) and garnish with fresh herbs. Serve hot, enjoying every bite filled with the flavors of autumn.

Tips for Preparation:

- For a richer flavor, add a splash of white wine to the sauce.
- Experiment with different types of nuts, such as hazelnuts or almonds, to create unique flavor and texture combinations.

Nutritional Value (per serving):

- Calories: about 400 kcal
- Proteins: 12 g
- Fats: 20 g
- Carbohydrates: 50 g
- Fiber: 5 g

Pumpkin pasta with nut sauce is not just dinner; it's a true culinary journey that will warm you up and fill your evening with the aromas and flavors of an autumn garden. Let this dish be your faithful companion on cool autumn evenings, bringing joy and coziness with every bite.

Autumn Vegetable Gratin with Cheese

Description: When the autumn evening descends, filling the air with coolness and the scent of fallen leaves, it is the perfect time for a cozy and warming dinner. Autumn vegetable gratin with cheese is not just a dish; it's true culinary magic that fills the home with the aromas of cheese and fresh herbs. Tender vegetables covered with a golden cheese crust create a harmony that turns an ordinary evening into a culinary adventure.

Ingredients:

- 1 sweet potato (sliced thinly)
- 1 zucchini (sliced thinly)
- 2 carrots (sliced thinly)
- 1 red bell pepper (sliced into strips)
- 1 onion (sliced into rings)
- 2 tablespoons olive oil
- 1 cup grated cheese (Gruyère, Cheddar, or Parmesan)
- 1/2 cup cream or milk
- 2 garlic cloves (minced)
- Salt and pepper to taste
- A pinch of ground nutmeg
- Fresh herbs (parsley or thyme) for garnish

Instructions:

1. **Preparing the Vegetables:**

o Preheat the oven to 200°C (400°F). Peel and thinly slice all the vegetables so they cook quickly and evenly.

2. **Preparing the Baking Dish:**
   o Grease a baking dish with olive oil. Layer the vegetable slices alternately for a beautiful effect. Lightly season each layer with salt and pepper.

3. **Making the Cream Mixture:**
   o In a small bowl, mix cream or milk with minced garlic, a pinch of nutmeg, salt, and pepper. Stir well to ensure all ingredients are evenly combined.

4. **Pouring and Topping with Cheese:**
   o Pour the prepared cream mixture over the layered vegetables. Sprinkle grated cheese on top, spreading it evenly over the surface.

5. **Baking the Gratin:**
   o Cover the dish with foil and bake in the preheated oven for about 30 minutes. Then remove the foil and bake for another 15-20 minutes until the cheese is golden and bubbly and the vegetables are tender.

6. **Serving:**
   o Remove the gratin from the oven and let it cool slightly. Serve hot, garnished with fresh herbs. This dish pairs wonderfully with a green salad or crusty bread.

Tips for Preparation:

- For a richer flavor, you can add some grated cheese or mustard to the cream mixture.
- Try using different types of cheese, such as feta or blue cheese, to create your unique combinations of flavors and textures.

Nutritional Value (per serving):

- Calories: about 350 kcal
- Proteins: 12 g
- Fats: 20 g
- Carbohydrates: 30 g
- Fiber: 5 g

Autumn vegetable gratin with cheese is not just dinner; it's a true culinary spell that will warm you up and fill the evening with the aromas and flavors of the autumn garden. Let this dish be your faithful companion on cool autumn evenings, bringing joy and comfort with every bite.

Section IV: Additional Spells

Magical Autumn Drinks

Autumn is when nature dons golden and crimson attire, and the cool evenings invite us to warm up by the hearth. During this season, it's especially delightful to enjoy a cup of fragrant beverage that not only warms but also brings a sense of coziness and tranquility. The magical drinks of September are not just beverages; they are true elixirs filled with the magic of autumn fruits and spices. Each sip of these drinks brings warmth and joy, infusing the day with magic.

Pumpkin Spice Latte

Description: Pumpkin spice latte is a true autumn classic, combining the creamy texture of milk, the rich flavor of pumpkin, and the aroma of spices. This drink brings a sense of coziness and warmth, even on the chilliest autumn days.

Ingredients:

- 1 cup milk (can use plant-based milk)
- 2 tablespoons pumpkin puree
- 1 tablespoon sugar (to taste)
- 1/2 teaspoon cinnamon
- 1/4 teaspoon nutmeg
- 1/4 teaspoon ginger
- 1/4 teaspoon cloves
- 1 shot of espresso or 1/2 cup strong coffee
- Whipped cream and cinnamon for garnish

Instructions:

1. **Prepare Pumpkin Milk:**

In a small saucepan over medium heat, combine the milk, pumpkin puree, and sugar. Stir constantly until the mixture is hot but not boiling.

Add Spices: Add the cinnamon, nutmeg, ginger, and cloves to the milk mixture. Stir well to combine.

Combine with Coffee: Prepare the espresso or strong coffee and add it to the milk mixture.

Serve: Pour the drink into a cup, top with whipped cream, and sprinkle with cinnamon.

Nutritional Information (per serving):

- Calories: 180 kcal
- Protein: 4 g
- Fat: 5 g
- Carbohydrates: 30 g
- Fiber: 2 g

Ginger and Honey Tea

Description: Ginger and honey tea is the perfect drink for chilly autumn evenings. Ginger warms and invigorates, while honey adds sweetness and soothes. This comforting beverage brings a cozy touch to your evening, combining the zesty kick of ginger with the calming essence of honey.

Ingredients:

- 1 liter of water
- 1 piece of fresh ginger (about 2 inches), sliced thinly
- 2 tablespoons honey
- 1 lemon, sliced
- 2-3 black or green tea bags (optional)

Instructions:

Boil Water:
In a large saucepan, bring the water to a boil. Add the sliced ginger and reduce the heat. Simmer on low heat for about 10 minutes.
Add Honey and Lemon:
Add the honey and lemon slices to the saucepan and stir well.
Steep Tea (Optional):
If desired, add the tea bags and let steep for 3-5 minutes, then remove them.
Strain and Serve:
Strain the tea and pour it into cups. Serve hot.

Nutritional Information (per serving):

- Calories: 60 kcal
- Protein: 0 g
- Fat: 0 g
- Carbohydrates: 16 g
- Fiber: 0 g

Apple Cider

Description: Apple cider is a drink that evokes the essence of autumn, apple orchards, and cozy family evenings. The natural flavor of apples, spiced with cinnamon and cloves, brings a sense of homey comfort.

Ingredients:

- 2 liters of apple juice (natural, unsweetened)
- 2 cinnamon sticks
- 5-6 whole cloves
- 1 orange, sliced
- 1 apple, sliced

Instructions:

Combine Ingredients: In a large pot, mix the apple juice, cinnamon sticks, and cloves. Bring to a boil over medium heat.

Simmer: Reduce the heat and add the sliced orange and apple. Simmer on low heat for about 30 minutes to blend all the flavors.

Strain and Serve: Strain the cider and pour it into cups. Serve hot, garnished with additional slices of orange or apple if desired.

Nutritional Information (per serving):

- Calories: 120 kcal
- Protein: 0 g
- Fat: 0 g
- Carbohydrates: 30 g
- Fiber: 1 g

These magical autumn drinks will fill your home with the aromas of the season and create an atmosphere of warmth and coziness. Let each sip remind you of nature's bounty and the magic of the fall season.

Autumn is the time when nature prepares for winter sleep, and we start seeking comfort and warmth in food. Healthy snacks help us not only to satisfy hunger between main meals but also to fill us with energy and joy. These snacks are made from natural ingredients that offer the generous autumn gifts of nature.

Honey and Dried Fruit Nut Bars

Nut bars are the perfect snack for those who love the combination of sweet and crunchy. These bars are not only delicious but also very nutritious, thanks to the nuts and dried fruits.

Ingredients:

- 1 cup oats
- 1/2 cup almonds (chopped)
- 1/2 cup walnuts (chopped)
- 1/2 cup dried fruits (raisins, dried apricots, prunes)
- 1/4 cup honey
- 1/4 cup natural peanut butter
- 1 teaspoon cinnamon

Instructions:

1. Preheat the oven to 180°C (350°F). Line a baking sheet with parchment paper.
2. In a large bowl, mix the oats, almonds, walnuts, and dried fruits.
3. In a small saucepan over low heat, melt the honey and peanut butter, then add the cinnamon. Stir well.
4. Pour the honey mixture into the nut mixture and mix thoroughly to ensure all ingredients are evenly coated.
5. Spread the mixture onto the prepared baking sheet and shape it into a rectangle. Bake for about 15-20 minutes, until the bars are golden.
6. Allow to cool, then cut into bars.

Nutritional Value (per serving):

- Calories: 200 kcal
- Protein: 5 g
- Fiber: 3 g
- Fat: 10 g
- Carbohydrates: 25 g

Honey and Nut Dried Fruits

Honey and nut dried fruits are a simple and delicious snack that can be prepared in just a few minutes. This snack is packed with vitamins and minerals to support health and energy.

Ingredients:

- 1 cup mixed dried fruits (apricots, raisins, dates)
- 1/2 cup walnuts
- 1/4 cup honey
- 1 teaspoon lemon juice

Instructions:

1. In a small bowl, mix the dried fruits and walnuts.
2. In another bowl, combine the honey and lemon juice. Pour the mixture over the dried fruits and nuts.
3. Stir well and let sit for a few minutes before serving.

Nutritional Value (per serving):

- Calories: 180 kcal
- Protein: 3 g
- Fat: 8 g
- Carbohydrates: 25 g
- Fiber: 4 g

Pine Nuts in Yogurt

Pine nuts in yogurt are the perfect snack for those seeking lightness and freshness. This snack is rich in protein and healthy fats that help maintain energy throughout the day.

Ingredients:

- 1 cup plain yogurt
- 1/4 cup pine nuts
- 1 tablespoon honey
- 1/2 teaspoon cinnamon

Instructions:

1. In a small bowl, mix the yogurt and honey.
2. Add the pine nuts and cinnamon. Stir well.
3. Serve in small cups or bowls.

Nutritional Value (per serving):

- Calories: 150 kcal
- Protein: 6 g
- Fat: 8 g
- Carbohydrates: 12 g
- Fiber: 1 g

These healthy snacks not only satisfy hunger but also fill us with the energy and vitamins needed to maintain health and vigor during autumn days. Let each of these snacks be your little magical moment, bringing joy and comfort.

Autumn is a time when nature's bounty is at its peak, offering an abundance of fruits and spices that inspire the creation of magical desserts. These sweet treats are not just delicious but also filled with the warmth and coziness that make autumn evenings special. Let's explore some enchanting dessert recipes that will fill your home with the irresistible aroma of fall.

Berry Mousse with Yogurt

Berry mousse is a light and airy dessert that will delight all berry lovers. It's not only delicious but also very healthy thanks to its natural ingredients.

Ingredients:

- 1 cup fresh or frozen berries (strawberries, raspberries, blueberries)
- 1 cup natural yogurt
- 2 tablespoons honey
- 1 teaspoon vanilla extract
- Mint leaves for garnish

Instructions:

1. In a blender, combine the berries, yogurt, honey, and vanilla extract until smooth.
2. Pour the mousse into serving glasses or bowls and chill in the refrigerator for at least 1 hour.
3. Serve garnished with mint leaves.

Nutritional Value (per serving):

- Calories: 100 kcal
- Protein: 5 g
- Fat: 2 g

- Carbohydrates: 15 g
- Fiber: 2 g

Fruit Salad with Nuts

Fruit salad is the perfect dessert for those who love fresh and juicy fruits. This salad is rich in vitamins and minerals that support health and energy.

Ingredients:

- 2 apples (diced)
- 2 pears (diced)
- 1 orange (peeled and segmented)
- 1/2 cup grapes (halved)
- 1/4 cup walnuts (toasted and chopped)
- 2 tablespoons honey
- Juice of 1 lemon

Instructions:

1. In a large bowl, combine the diced apples, pears, orange segments, and grapes.
2. In a small bowl, mix honey and lemon juice. Drizzle the mixture over the fruits and toss well to combine.
3. Add the chopped walnuts and toss again.
4. Serve the salad chilled.

Nutritional Information (per serving):

- Calories: 150 kcal
- Protein: 2 g
- Fat: 6 g
- Carbohydrates: 25 g
- Fiber: 4 g

Baked Pears with Honey and Cinnamon

- 4 pears (halved and cored)
- 2 tablespoons honey
- 1 teaspoon cinnamon
- 1/4 cup walnuts (toasted and chopped)

Instructions:

1. Preheat your oven to 180°C (350°F). Place the pear halves on a baking sheet lined with parchment paper.
2. Drizzle each pear half with honey and sprinkle with cinnamon.
3. Bake the pears in the preheated oven for about 20 minutes, until they become soft.
4. Serve the pears warm, sprinkled with chopped walnuts.

Nutritional Value (per serving):

- Calories: 120 kcal
- Protein: 1 g
- Fat: 3 g
- Carbohydrates: 25 g
- Fiber: 4 g

These light and healthy desserts will fill your home with the aromas of autumn and create a warm and cozy atmosphere. Let each of these desserts be your little magical moment, bringing joy and delight.

Autumn Path to Health

Ways of Autumn Magic

Autumn is not only a time to enjoy the bounty of nature but also to rethink our lifestyle and diet. As the cool days and cozy evenings arrive, we seek warmth and comfort, and that's where the magic of autumn lies. This book has become a guide to the world of healthy and delicious recipes that will help you not only maintain your health but also enjoy every meal.

Healthy eating is not just about what we eat but also how we eat it. By savoring each dish, you immerse yourself in the process, experiencing the aromas and flavors that bring joy and satisfaction. Let each recipe in this book become a little magical ritual that brings happiness and strengthens your health.

Let this autumn be the beginning of your journey to health and well-being. Start your day with pumpkin and cinnamon pancakes, enjoy a lunch of pumpkin soup with ginger and coconut milk, and in the evening, immerse yourself in the warmth and comfort of cooking a gratin of autumn vegetables with cheese. Every recipe is a step towards a new level of health and happiness

It's important to remember that healthy eating is not about strict restrictions and avoiding favorite foods. It's about balance, moderation, and choosing quality and beneficial ingredients. Autumn offers a wealth of flavors and textures, and we can use these gifts from nature to make our lives healthier and more joyful.

May this book inspire you to create your own culinary masterpieces, to experiment with new ingredients and flavors. Let each recipe be a starting point for your culinary creativity, filling your life with the magic of autumn.

Acknowledgements

The creation of this book has been a journey filled with joy, discoveries, and inspiration. First and foremost, I want to thank nature for its generous gifts, which made the creation of these amazing and healthy recipes possible. Each fruit, vegetable, and grain adds its unique note to the symphony of autumn flavors.

I would like to express special gratitude to my grandmother, whose recipes and stories about culinary traditions became the foundation of this book. Her love for cooking and caring for the family inspired me to create these recipes, filled with warmth and comfort.

Thank you to my family and friends who supported me at every stage of creating this book. Their love and support helped me overcome difficulties and continue working on the project, believing in its success. They were my first tasters and critics, and their honest feedback helped make each dish better.

A huge thank you to my team, without whom this book would not have been possible. Your hard work, talent, and dedication made the creation of this book possible.

Thank you to my readers who chose this book. I hope it becomes a source of inspiration and joy for you, helps you discover new horizons in cooking, and makes your autumn season healthier and more delicious. May each recipe in this book bring you pleasure and happiness, filling your home with the aromas and warmth of autumn.

Helpful Resources

If you enjoyed the recipes and tips from this book, I invite you to explore my other works. In them, you will find even more inspiration for creating delicious and healthy dishes that will help you maintain your health and enjoy every meal.

My books are available on Amazon. You can find them on my author page at the following link:

https://www.amazon.com/stores/Yurii-Sreda/author/B0CSFS13NB?ref=ap_rdr&isDramIntegrated=true&shoppingPortalEnabled=true

Each of my books offers a unique approach to healthy eating and cooking. I hope they become a valuable resource and source of inspiration for you, helping to make your life healthier and more delicious.

If you found value in this book, please consider leaving a review on Amazon. Your support through reviews helps us reach more people who might benefit from this guide.
To do this, scan this QR code and fill out all the fields of the form, then click submit.

https://www.amazon.com/review/create-review/?ie=UTF8&channel=glance-detail&asin=B0DBW4Y5ZQ

With respect and warmth, Yurii Sreda

Yurii & Inna Sreda

Transformative Nutrition:
Comprehensive Guides to Healthy Eating,
Weight Loss, and Sustainable Wellness

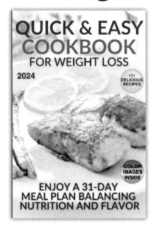

Find more books on the author's page here

Made in the USA
Las Vegas, NV
30 October 2024